Pipeline Productions presents

MONSTERING THE ROCKETMAN

by **Henry Naylor**

Monstering the Rocketman premiered at the Pleasance Ace Dome at the Edinburgh Festival Fringe on 30 July 2025.

The play transferred to Arcola Theatre, London, on 3 February 2026.

MONSTERING THE ROCKETMAN

by **Henry Naylor**

LYNX	Henry Naylor
Director/Dramaturg	Darren Lee Cole
AV Designer	Iain Pearson
Producer	Henry Naylor

Monstering the Rocketman will have a national tour of the UK in autumn 2026, which will be produced by Makin Projects. Tour dates will be announced on: **www.henrynaylor.com**

The *Monstering* team would like to thank Mark and Penny Makin for arranging the *MTR* 2026 autumn tour. You can contact Mark through the Makin Projects website:
www.makinprojects.co.uk

BIOGRAPHIES

HENRY NAYLOR | LYNX / WRITER / PRODUCER

Yorkshireman Henry Naylor is a leading playwright on the international fringe circuit.

A former head writer on *Spitting Image*, he typically focuses on current affairs and the impact of major global events upon ordinary people. Blending humour with tragedy – and often stand-up with drama – he tackles the nuances of international politics.

A successful comedian for many years, Naylor shared a double-act with Andy Parsons. They hosted nine series of the weekly topical comedy *Parsons & Naylor's Pullout Sections* on BBC Radio 2. After working as a writer and cameo performer on leading TV comedies such as *Smith & Jones*, *Weekending*, *The Lenny Henry Show*, *Goodness Gracious Me*, *Saturday Night Live*, *Hale & Pace*, *Alistair MacGowan's Big Impression*, *Dead Ringers*, and *Headcases*, Naylor switched from comedy to drama.

Inspired by a harrowing trip to the Afghan warzone (retold in *Afghanistan Is Not Funny*), Naylor began writing plays about the West's clumsy relationship with the Middle East – notably in his acclaimed *Arabian Nightmares* series: *The Collector*, *Echoes*, *Angel* and *The Nights*.

Other plays have also tackled contentious news themes such as the refugee crisis, the care homes disaster and antisemitism (in *Borders*, *Let the Bodies Pile* and *Games*).

Subsequently, he has become one of the most decorated playwrights on the international indie scene, winning 56 awards and nominations, including main prizes at the Edinburgh, Adelaide, Hollywood, New York IFES and Prague Fringes.

Naylor has won the Fringe First an astonishing four times – and, uniquely, he won the Adelaide Critics' Overall Award three years running. Other highlights include a nomination for France's Globe de Cristal and *The Times* naming *Angel* as a 'Play of the Year.'

There have been almost 2000 public performances of his work, which has played in five continents and has been translated into fifteen languages.

DARREN LEE COLE | DIRECTOR / DRAMATURG

Darren is a leading producer-director off-Broadway, having been the Artistic Director of the famous SoHo Playhouse since 2004. The list of his credits is awe-inspiring, and very, very long– but his favourite projects have included producing: Hannah Gadsby's *Nanette*; Phoebe Waller-Bridge in *Fleabag*; *Daniel Sloss: X*; *TJ & Dave*; *The Old Man and the Old Moon* with PigPen Theatre Co.; *Killer Joe* by Tracy Letts (Vaudville Theatre, West End, London, SoHo Playhouse NYC & The Theatre Chicago); *The Emperor Jones* (w/Irish Rep); and *Laticia* at Théâtre Espace Marais, Paris. Directing credits: *Games*; *Rap Guide Series* with Baba Brinkman (*Consciousness, Religion, Climate Chaos, Canterbury Tales, Culture*); *Jamaica Farewell* and *The Actor's Nightmare*. Mr Cole is also the Artistic Director and Producer of the Fringe Encore Series: fringeencoreseries.com.

IAIN PEARSON | AV DESIGNER

Iain is an audio visual designer based in Glasgow, with over ten years' experience in theatrical production design, combining his skills with sound, lights and projection in a number of shows, including *Afghanistan Is Not Funny* (2023), *Let the Bodies Pile* (2024) and *Bethlehem Calling* (2025).

ACCEPTABLE IN THE EIGHTIES
Henry Naylor

It's human to remember the best bits of the past, and edit out the worst.
Currently there's a lot of nostalgia for the 1980s.
Beneath the gaudy clothes, the big hair and even bigger shoulder pads was a darker, more scary, more violent country.
There was football hooliganism, race riots, IRA bombs, the poll tax revolts, lengthy dole queues and crippling, brutal strikes.
It was a time of massive social upheaval, as Britain strove to define itself.
Not everyone felt truly safe in the eighties.

I've been wanting to write a series of plays about the decade for a while.
If nothing else, to contradict the demagogues selling us a romanticised view of the past. For research, I spent four months in the British Library reading back issues of the tabloids, to revisit and understand the mindset of the 1980s.

This was a golden era for the tabloids, and *The Sun* was the backdrop of our lives.
As the biggest-selling daily newspaper in the English-speaking world, it sold nearly five million copies a day, with a readership of some twelve million people.
It was seen on every train carriage, on every bus – it even wrapped our fish and chip suppers. Impossible to avoid its bold, provocative, sometimes hilarious, often offensive headlines.

Reading those papers today is alarming. We often lambast the society of today for being intolerant, but we've come a long way. Intolerance and hate speech were mainstream in the eighties, and racist terms were commonplace. The French were 'Frogs,' the Germans 'Krauts' and the Japanese 'Japs.' Black faces rarely appeared on the front pages and when they did, they were usually those of criminals. But the greatest invective was reserved for the gay community, for this was the height of the AIDS crisis, and the tabloids wanted a scapegoat.

When the Chief Constable of Greater Manchester, James Anderton, an evangelical Christian, spoke to a national conference about how the police should deal with AIDS, he said: 'Everywhere I go I see evidence of people swirling around in the cesspool of their own making. Why do homosexuals freely engage in sodomy and other obnoxious sexual practices knowing the dangers involved?'

He was dismissed as a crank by the broadsheets. Not so by *The Sun*. In an editorial it declared that it 'hopes Mr Anderton will treat these perverts with the contempt they deserve'.

Coverage was relentless and overwhelmingly negative, with headlines that are shocking to modern eyes: for instance, 'Gays are Plague In Our Midst', 'MI6 Boss was Poof', etc. And you might be forgiven for thinking that the tabloids saw it as a moral duty to 'out' gay celebrities and portray them as sexual deviants. There was a particular fascination with celebrity/rent boy stories. Russell Harty had his career destroyed in such a way, and Harvey Proctor too.

And then came Elton John. You could almost smell the glee of *Sun* editor Kelvin MacKenzie when he was offered the 'confessions' of a male prostitute known as 'American Barry'. MacKenzie has admitted some stories were 'too good to check,' and this was one of them. He published. Disastrously, he was to discover that 'Barry' was a liar. He was neither American, nor called 'Barry'. He was called 'Stephen' and worked in a dry-cleaners in Twyford, and had made the whole thing up. Elton was understandably incensed. He wasn't in Britain when the alleged orgies took place. He wasn't even in the same continent. He was in the States having a costume fitting, and he had the taxi receipts to prove it.

As a member of *The Sunday Times* 100 Rich List, Elton had the money and the resources to fight. He also had the time, as he was taking a year's sabbatical to rest his damaged vocal cords.

But when Elton sued, MacKenzie refused to back down. Instead of admitting his mistake, he doubled down on the lie and relentlessly pursued the star…

An extraordinary tale ensued, which forms the subject of *Monstering the Rocketman*. It involves Ferraris, punch-ups, bugged phone calls, Sarah Ferguson, Duchess of York, Michael Parkinson, the Vice Squad and a pair of 'devil dogs'. It resulted in Elton settling for a whopping one million pounds of damages, still the largest libel payout in British history.

In an era when the tabloids were all about making money, this was a salutary lesson. I believe it was a turning point in British history, for good and bad. On the positive side, I believe the press had to become more sensitive to minorities, which paved the way for our more diverse and tolerant Britain. On the negative side was the damage to the reputation of the media.

Elton's was one of a series of high-profile legal cases and payouts by the tabloids.
In 1987–88 alone, the Queen was paid £100k by *The Sun*; Koo Stark £300k by the *Mail on Sunday*; Jeffrey Archer £500k by *The Star*.
By the end of the decade, the credibility of the print media was in shreds.
In 1990 a survey concluded that only fourteen per cent of the British public had confidence in the British press.
Today, after the hacking scandals, that figure stands at thirteen per cent. The damage was done long before.
A tragedy for us all.

It's easy to criticise the tabloids.
But we, the public, played our part. We were willing to pay for thrilling stories – regardless of whether they were true or not. How else to explain the phenomenon of the *Sunday Sport*, known for headlines like 'Aliens Turned Our Son Into a Fish Finger', 'Donkey Robs Bank' and 'World War II Bomber Found on the Moon'. Its readers surely knew they were being deceived, but they didn't seem to mind just so long as the storylines were compelling.
So who would blame the eighties popular press editors for 'hyping up', 'sexing up' and even 'making up' stories? That was what we, the public, seemed to be demanding.

In a time of screaming TikTok influencers, vacuous Only-Fans-narcissists and demagogues with orange faces, we need a strong, trustworthy source of Truth.
If nothing else, to dismiss the 'alternative facts' and 'firehose of falsehoods' corroding our democracy, and to stop us from retweeting the BS fed to us by bots.

The Free Press is surely the answer. It needs to be powerful, have free rein, but above all be responsible. That can only be achieved by acknowledging the mistakes of the past, and by examining where the trust was lost: in the mid-eighties, when Profits were placed before Truth. It can be done, but as Elton has said, sorry seems to be the hardest word.

This article was originally published in Scotland on Sunday, *August 2025*

arcola theatre

ABOUT THE ARCOLA

Arcola produces daring, high-quality theatre in the heart of East London and beyond.

We create trailblazing shows for all.

Arcola commissions and premieres exciting, original works alongside rare gems of world drama and bold new productions of classics.

Our socially engaged, international programme champions diversity, challenges the status quo, and attracts over 65,000 people to our building each year.

Ticket prices are some of the most affordable in London, and our long-running Pay-What-You-Can scheme ensures there is no financial barrier to accessing the theatre.

We enable new and diverse talent.

Arcola platforms and empowers the next generation in theatre.

Since opening in 2000, we have supported thousands of people – on stage, backstage and front of house – to develop their skills and careers. Alecky Blythe, Rebecca Lenkiewicz and Barney Norris' first plays were produced at Arcola. Arinzé Kene started acting in our youth theatre; Wunmi Mosaku made her stage debut here. Aml Ameen, Zawe Ashton, Mike Bartlett, Polly Findlay, Lucy Kirkwood, Lynette Linton, Michael Longhurst and Lyndsey Turner all worked at Arcola at the start of their careers.

Our annual Grimeborn festival unlocks opera for everybody. We give young and diverse companies a platform to embark on bold artistic ventures. Contemporary stagings and affordable ticket prices make opera accessible for the many.

Arcola Academy empowers young people to build their futures within the arts and explore theatre and performance as a professional pathway.

Through ArcolaLAB we offer 26 weeks of free rehearsal space every year to culturally diverse and refugee artists. In 2017, we won the UK Theatre Award for Promotion of Diversity.

We expand opportunities for everyone to make theatre.

Arcola Participation creates thousands of creative opportunities every year for the people of Hackney and beyond – including through our youth theatre, and pioneering Queer, ages 50+, and Mental Health community companies. Every year, we showcase original productions by these companies in our Participation Festival. In 2017 we won the Adiaha Antigha Award for Most Imaginative Approach to Outreach.

We imagine and build a sustainable future.

Arcola aims to be the world's first carbon-neutral theatre. Our environment sustainability-initiatives, developed with our sister company Arcola Energy, are internationally renowned. In 2018 we won The Stage Sustainability Award in recognition of our ongoing attempts to reduce carbon emissions and raise awareness of climate emergency.

'Arcola Theatre brings the very best of the world's performing and visual arts to the people of the world living and working in London'
Guardian

'Arcola is one of the great success stories of the British Theatre'
The Stage

THANKS TO

Sean Gascoine and Annie Shipton at United Agents – for being an all-round pair of legends.

Paul Sullivan for his typical PR brilliance.

Enormously indebted, to Rosalind Furlong who took the superb publicity shots. Fab as ever.

Steve Ullathorne for taking the excellent production stills.

Laura Oates – just for being Lovely Laura Oates – and for her brilllance with props and costumes.

Viv, Danny, Leo and Sarah, of course.

Massive thanks to the OSO Arts Centre in Barnes and Lydia Sax, for making me their Artist-in-Residence while I developed the show.

Mike Blaha has been brilliant as ever, taking a very different version of the show to the Hollywood Fringe for three work-in-progress performances!

Anthony Alderson and his team at the Pleasance, for our premiere season.

Everybody at Arcola – there's so many to thank here – but especial thanks to Leyla and Mehmet, General Manager Charlotte Croft, Artistic Associate and Producer Katharine Farmer, Sarah Colson and Ella Muir in Marketing, and Technical Manager Glenford Barnes.

Mark and Penny at Makin Projects have been great sorting out the tour.

And everyone at Nick Hern Books – including Commissioning Editor Maddie Hindes, Production Controller Beth Archer, and Nick himself!

H.N.

OTHER PLAYS BY HENRY NAYLOR

The Collector premiered at the Gilded Balloon in 2014, it told the story of a translator in an Abu Ghraib-style jail and won a Fringe First.

Echoes controversially compared jihadi brides to pioneers of the Victorian Empire. The first play to be staged about ISIS on a British stage, it won numerous international awards, including Overall Best Theatre at Adelaide.

Selected for the Brits Off Broadway season, it played for a month at New York's 59E59. There have been many international productions of the show. Pinchforn's version played at Madrid's 760-seater Teatro Espanōl and was described by ABC Spain as a 'a major work of art: major in its writing, in its dramatic power.'

Angel was about a Kurdish sniper during the Siege of Kobane. Performed by the exceptional Filipa Bragança, it secured another Fringe First, sold out its entire Edinburgh run, and was selected as one of *The Times'* Best Plays of the Year. Subsequently it has been translated into thirteen different languages, and award-winning productions have been staged in five continents. There have been over 500 public performances of the show. The Parisian production ran for three months at Théâtre Tristan Bernard and won the Globe De Cristal (France's equivalent of the Golden Globes) with actress Lina El Arabi.

Borders grappled with the refugee crisis. It contrasted the life of a paparazzo with that of a Syrian graffiti artist, resulting in a spectacular climax when they collide in the Mediterranean Sea. It won both a Fringe First and the Carol Tambor Best of Edinburgh Award and ran for a month at the Theatre Next Door in New York. There have been numerous international productions of the play – one in Belgium even flooded the stage for the climax!! – our heroine was literally swimming for her life! A major Spanish tour of show begins in Bilbao in May 2026.

Games marked Henry's first departure from Middle Eastern subject matter and was also his first collaboration with Darren Lee Cole. It told the tragic true story of the two Jewish athletes who were selected for Hitler's 1936 Olympic squad. An attack on racial discrimination, it was written at the time of the Labour Party's antisemitism scandal. Winning Henry's third Overall Critics' Choice Award at the Adelaide Fringe, it went on to play for almost two months at the SoHo Playhouse in New York. ShowScore consistently rated it in the 'Top Three Off-Broadway shows.'

The Nights is a horror story, set in a military memorabilia shop. The creepy shopkeeper gradually reveals his violent past in a brutal climax. Released at the time of Covid – it has only toured once internationally, to the Adelaide Fringe, where it picked up a Critics' Choice Award.

Afghanistan Is Not Funny was Henry and Darren's second collaboration. Henry himself recounted the true story of his 2002 trip to the Afghan warzone, in which he was captured by the mujhadheen. The show toured for two years – including a major tour of India – and won numerous international awards, including both the Platinum Medal and Best International at the Hollywood Fringe, and the Outstanding Production Award at the 'Best of All the Fests', the International Fringe Encore Series New York.

Let the Bodies Pile starred Emily Carding. She played two roles – that of a nurse in a care home during the Covid crisis, and also the daughter of a woman murdered by Harold Shipman. It was nominated for the Creative Award at Prague.

ENQUIRIES
To check Henry's availability as a writer or performer – or writer-performer – contact Henry's agent, Sean Gascoine at United Agents. He also arranges the licensing of Henry's back catalogue of work:
sgascoine@unitedagents.co.uk

STAY IN TOUCH!
You can stay in touch with Henry and his work via…
www.henrynaylor.com
Instagram: naylor.henry
X: @HenryNaylorUK
Facebook: www.facebook.com/henry.naylor.75

MONSTERING THE ROCKETMAN

Henry Naylor

This play is dedicated to LO

Character

LYNX

This text went to press before the end of rehearsals and so may differ slightly from the play as performed.

A slide as the audience comes in, reading:

*'Tom Petrie [Sun News Editor] used to come into my office…
and would tell me some incredible story.
I would say: "But is it true?"
Tom would look at me, then I would say,
"You know, Tom, I think this one is too true to check",
and then we would publish it, because it sounded true!
This didn't happen once, it happened loads of times…'*

[*Kelvin MacKenzie, interviewed in the* Press Gazette, *2006*]

—

Hold a cool-clear drink of water, Pure as Truth.
Add a single drip of ink.
Watch: as it unfurls complex tentacles, reaching, stretching like an octopus cloud.
A single drop of ink won't taste good – but it won't harm you.
But add another. And another. And…
How many drops before it becomes Toxic?
Poisonous?
Deadly?

—

This is a tabloid story from the 1980s.
And because it's a tabloid story from the eighties, most of it is untrue.
Exaggerated, made up.
But like all the best lies – it's sprinkled with truths.
To give it the appearance of authenticity.

But: where is the line between fact and fiction?
Not our concern.
Truth is just a commodity to be sold…

—

...*The Sun* rises and sets in a brutalist building in Wapping.

At night, when the presses roll, the whole building shakes with their ferocity.
The Power of the Press is real: tangible.
An energy which enters your body, vibrates every cell.
Irresistible, intoxicating. Seductive.

Five million copies printed hastily.
The ink: made of carbon black and mineral oil.
No time to dry, on cheap, poorly absorbent paper;
still damp when it hits the morning news-stands.
The words transfer to readers' fingers.
The grime passed to their faces.
For the rest of the day, twelve million readers wear the smuts and smears of *The Sun* like a second skin: a stain.

Follow me down the seventh-floor corridor...
Iconic front pages blown large.
The headlines; small masterpieces of wit and economy.
Remember a headline from the eighties? – and it'll be a *Sun* headline.
When Lib Dems leader Paddy Ashdown was caught screwing his secretary: 'Paddy Pants-Down';
when George Michael was caught soliciting in a public toilet: 'Zip Me Up Before You Go-Go';
but others, more shocking: when hundreds died in a sinking Argentinan warship: 'Gotcha'.

Now pause before the newsroom door. Above, a sign declaring, 'Welcome to *Sun* Country'.

This is how it sees itself. A 'country'.
A state within a state.
A British Vatican.
With its own laws, its own jurisdiction.
This country is no Democracy. It is a Dictatorship, with a cult of personality – that of its editor, the most powerful man in Britain:

Kelvin MacKenzie.
He chooses governments, picks prime ministers, turns football managers into vegetables.
Shapes the narrative of a nation.

...And in February 1987, he's leaping up and down, yelling 'Fuck me. Ring the klaxon. It's a Ferret...'

If a story's a Ferret, it's so exciting, it makes the reader hop around like they have a ferret down their trousers.

'No, no – it's more than that – it's a Double Ferret... In fact this is more than THAT – this is a – this is a – '
Kelvin turns to his senior journalists.
Addresses a woman with enormous spectacles, alarming bright lipstick and a voice grated by a million cigarettes.
'Come on, Joan, you're a fucking writer, what's the collective noun of fucking ferrets?'
'It's a "Business" of Fucking Ferrets, Kelvin.'
'This is a Fucking "Business" of Fucking Ferrets!!'
Joan sighs inwardly; she's seen this before:
'But is it true, Kelvin?'

...She's talking to the wrong man.
Kelvin has recently printed a story called 'Freddie Starr Ate My Hamster'.
He's presided over a massive rise in circulation.
He's untouchable.
'"Is it true? Is it true?"' He mocks.
'You want to print the unverified story of a drug-taking rent boy??'
'It SOUNDS fucking true.'
'It's Elton John, Kelvin!'
'Exactly! The most famous star on the fucking planet! The only man who appears on the front pages – as a rockstar – and the back – as chairman of Watford Football Club.'
'He's the most litigious man in Britain.'
'Fuck him... PRINT IT.'

—

February twenty-fifth, seven a.m.

Hurrying to work.
Can't be late: my first week at *The Sun*; trying to impress.

...Snatch a copy of our paper from the news-stand,
Board the Tube to Wapping...

…still wearing last night's suit.
Hadn't time to go home or take a shower.
So sprayed myself with a can of Lynx.
Clothes and all.
May have overdone it…
…I'm soon to find out what the 'Lynx Effect' really is, as my fellow passengers back away holding their noses.
And I now have my own seat on a crowded commute…
Result!

Flicking through the paper, looking for my name.

All I want is a byline…
My name in print.

Just the one so far.
A story about the love life of the bloke who plays Mr Blobby entitled 'Blobby Blobby Blobby's on the Jobby'.
Wasn't going to win a Pulitzer, let's be honest…
But I'm on a week-long trial and a couple more of those might land me a staff contract.

And as Dad always used to say – 'You don't become a foreign correspondent overnight:
you have to serve your time. Get a job in the dailies, get practice in reporting.'
Sound advice.
Although I doubt why an interview with Mr Blobby is preparing me for conflabs with world leaders. Even if he does talk more sense than Margaret Thatcher: 'Blobby Blobby Blobby'.

Scanning the paper, looking for yesterday's work…
I'd been reporting on the Rear of the Year ceremony – the prize for Britain's Best Bum –
which had been won by *EastEnders'* Anita Dobson, thirty-nine…
a triumph which she'd celebrated like the Nobel Peace Prize.
After I'd filed my copy, I was invited to celebrate with her team, long into the night at Stringfellows.
Hence the Lynx: to disguise the after-club kebab.

There! Page eleven!
Under the headline 'Rear Enders': big picture of Dobson waving her triumphant arse.

Next to it, a starburst: 'Angie's Botty Drives Us All Potty'.
But it's all picture; just a couple of lines of my text…
Too short.
Fuck!
No byline.
Fuck.
Fuck.

I toss the paper onto the empty seat next to me, in disgust.

Now look around the train carriage.
Big hair, big shoulder pads and even bigger pay packets.
No faces, no eyes. Only copies of my paper.
With its headline: 'ELTON IN VICE BOY SCANDAL'.

All of us with ink on our fingers.

—

Ten thousand miles away, in Sydney's Sebel hotel, rocker Elton, thirty-nine, has no voice…
He's overdone it on his Australian tour.
In the middle of one of his four-hour concerts, his voice disappeared.
Leaving him flapping his mouth soundlessly on stage, like his nemesis, 'The Mime Artist' Madonna.

The experts say the career-threatening nodules on his throat aren't cancer.
And he should recover if he rests his voice, for a year…

In his darker moments he's been wondering who he might become if he doesn't recover…
An identity crisis compounded by the fact that, in one month, he'll reach the watershed of forty.
Who should he be for the rest of his life?

The phone rings. It's his mum.
'Mum, I told you not to call. I have to rest my voice.'
'Did you do it, Reg?'
Elton sighs inwardly. Even now, she still calls him 'Reg'. For the ten-millionth time in his life, he croaks, 'Mum, it's "ELTON". Did I do "what"?'

"'Recline on a bed in skimpy leather shorts, looking 'like Cleopatra', twirling a sex aid between your fingers"?'

Elton shrieks and puts his recovery back by three weeks...

He gets London to fax him the story; it's a lively fiction.
A prostitute called American Barry proclaims to have recruited teenagers for Elton's 'bizarre drugs and vice orgies'...

Elton needs advice – so calls his Write-Hand Man, lyricist Bernie Taupin.
'Bernie!'
Bernie Taupin was raised in rural Lincolnshire – but has lived in the States for ten years; he speaks like a northern farmer, but with an American accent.
(*Bernie speaks in American accent throughout.*) ''Ow do, Elton.'
'Bernie! – Do I resemble Cleopatra??'
'Does age not wither you, nor custom stale your infinite variety?'
'No.'
'Then why you asking?'
'The papers are saying I looked like "Cleopatra twirling a sex aid, screwing rent boys in leather shorts".'
'Fucking Nora!!! Is it true?'
'Course it isn't true. I wouldn't be seen dead in leather shorts'...
'You're not going to sue, are you, pal?'
'They're going to run and run this – tomorrow: "Elton's tutu party".'
'I'd forget it. It'll be chip paper in the morning.'

Chip paper...
'Elton in Vice Boy Scandal': wrapping the nation's favourite meal.
The nation enjoying their favourite food on a bed of 'Elton in Vice Boy Scandal'.
Diners with grease and smuts of tabloid ink on their fingers.
Licking their fingers clean, ingesting the Words of *The Sun*.
Feasting on the reputation of Elton John.

'I'm suing.'

After Elton's team issues the first writ, they phone *The Sun*'s rivals, the *Daily Mirror*...

The *Mirror* had been the world's bestselling daily.
But *The Sun* stole that title in 1978, and they're desperate for revenge.

Elton gives them taxi receipts proving he was four thousand miles away when the alleged 'orgy' took place...
The *Mirror* prints them on the front page and accuses *The Sun* of 'Lies'.

Kelvin, unrepentant, responds with a headline of his own:
'YOU'RE a Liar, Elton',
then prints a second set of American Barry's revelations.

...which prompts another phone call to Australia.
'Did you do it, Reg?'
'"Elton", Mum... Did I do "what"?'
'Have "pink tutu parties with tattooed punks with spikey hair"?'
Elton shrieks and sets back his recovery by six more months.

—

Even before my dad was killed, I wanted to be a journalist.
He'd already persuaded me of the glamour of the profession, returning from foreign fields with unsuitable presents.
A gold bullet from Uganda. A Soviet gas mask from Afghanistan...
Battle souvenirs which created new conflicts, on a domestic front – with my mother.
'Why would a ten-year-old boy want a curved sword belonging to the Shah of Iran??'
What ten-year old boy WOULDN'T want a curved sword belonging to the Shah of Iran??

After Mum's successful campaign of unilateral disarmament, Dad would take me aside, tell me conspiratorially of meetings with monsters, powwows with presidents.

'Are the Russians bad people, Dad?'
'No. They have reasons for doing what they do.'
'So why do you say they are?'
'There are a million angles to every story. If you want longevity in this career – you got to give your editor what he wants.'

The editor came before everything: his family, his marriage, even his own life...

The editor sent him to Soweto, where I was orphaned by a stray bullet.

But my course was already set.
That's why I find myself, aged twenty-two, a cub reporter for a national paper.
Trying to make a dead man proud.

—

'FALL IN, TROOPS.'
'Commander' Petrie, the news editor, summons his team to the daily news conference using a megaphone.
He's an ex-serviceman – hence the nickname – and much of his language is military in tone...

Journalists are expected to bring story ideas to conference.
With just one byline in a week, I need to do something radical.
Perhaps celebrity stories aren't my forte.
Could try something different; no one's writing about the destruction of the Brazilian rainforests.
There's a gap I can fill.

Joan sits noisily in the chair next to me.
'Oh my God! What do you smell like??'
'Lynx.'
'My son wears that. Not sure whether it's Eau de Toilette or Toilet Odour. Don't stand too close to a naked flame, is all I can say; you'll probably catch fire... I'm Joan, by the way. Should I bother learning your name?'
'What does that mean?'
'Most temps don't survive the week. They don't understand this paper. Once, an idiot tried to pitch stories about the Brazilian rainforests. Hahaha.'
I look with horror at my story ideas.
'Oh my God, Lynx. Do you actually want people to read your work? Or do you want to go and write for the *Guardian*?'
'What's wrong with the *Guardian*?'

'The *Sunday Sport* sells more copies than the *Guardian*. The public would rather read a story about "Adolf Hitler Being a Woman" or "World War II Bombers on the Moon" than a lecture on South American woodland. You're in the entertainment business, now.'
A surge of panic: 'Shit, Joan! I've nothing to pitch.'
'Don't worry, Lynx; I'll see you through.'

'AT EASE.'
Still using the megaphone, Petrie starts the meeting: 'LADIES AND GENTLEMEN. WE'RE UNDER ATTACK.'
Then raises the *Mirror*'s front page.
The headline: 'THE BIG LIE'.
'SEEMS ELTON IS WORKING WITH THE ENEMY. HE'S GIVEN THEM HIS TAXI RECEIPTS TO PROVE HE WAS IN NEW YORK... THIS IS WAR.'
Joan rolls her eyes: 'Don't tell me that all we've got is the account of a drug-taking rent boy; don't tell me Kelvin thought this story was "too good to check"?'
Petrie lowers the megaphone helplessly. 'He wants us to stand this story up. I need volunteers to do the legwork. Any takers?'
Joan digs me in the ribs.
I raise my hand. 'Er, me.'

The chairs squeal, conference is over.
I turn to Joan, ask, 'Do you think Elton did it?'
'Almost certainly not. "American Barry" isn't the most credible source. He's neither American, nor called Barry... He's called Stephen and he works for a dry-cleaner's in Twyford.'
'So why don't we just admit our mistake?'
'You are funny, Lynx! Can't possibly admit we're wrong. Not now the *Mirror* is fighting us... Now, go and stand this story up.'
I feel a confusion of panic.
'Where do I begin?'
'Find the prostitutes American Barry recruited, interview them, and get them to back up his story.'
'How?'
'Read the report, Lynx! He made his recruits at the Apollo Club: start there.'

'Right.'
'And before you go – go to the Picture Desk; borrow the picture of American Barry – might jog some memories. But DON'T LOSE that picture. It's an exclusive.'

—

The Apollo Club is a gloomy 'Members' Club' in Soho, with blacked-out windows and sticky carpets.
This is the era of AIDS. I'd been told that these were hard times for the vice industry. Thought it'd be empty.
But the bar is heaving.
I see one young guy, early forties, who seems to be eating a boiled sweet.
He's flirting with the barman when I interrupt, and show him the picture of American Barry.
'Excuse me, you look like a regular… do you know this guy? Goes by the name of American Barry?'
'He's a young fella, in'he?'
'He claims he pimped for Elton.'
'Ah! Is he the one from Kettleborough?'
'Twyford.'
'Twyford, ah! Yeah, I've heard of him… What's it worth?'
I slip him fifty quid. 'So what can you tell me?'
'Apparently *The Sun* paid him two thousand quid for his story… And he's fucked me.'
'Really???'
He starts pointing out his fellow drinkers. 'And he's fucked him… And he's fucked him… He's fucked most people in this bar actually.'
'Huh??'
'…By selling his story exclusively to *The Sun*. Our editors have all given us a right bollocking for not getting the story first.'
'You're a journalist??'
'Steve Pink, *Daily Mirror*. EVERYONE in here is a journalist.'
The drinkers nod in agreement.
'Yeah, I'm a journalist.'
'Me, too.'
'A journalist.'
'Journalist.'

…As the press pack launches its very own 'I Am Spartacus'
I turn to Pink and ask:
'What are you all doing in a sex dungeon?'
'Same as you: researching American Barry.'
'Give me that fifty quid back!'
'Too late – you're getting the first round in.' Pink hands the cash to the barman: 'Mine's an IPA.'
'Rotten bastard!!'
While I try to recover the cash from the barman, Pink slips out of the bar…
…With the American Barry photo.
I realise too late.
Rush into the stairwell.
Empty.
Fuck.
My heart sinks.
Fuck.
I was here to find an exclusive story. Instead I've handed our deadliest opponent our exclusive picture.
And I told him American Barry was from Twyford.
Pink is probably pounding the pavements up there already.
I groan, slump against the wall, head in hands…
…When I realise someone is standing above me.
A man with a goatee beard.
'Did I hear it right, that *The Sun* paid two thousand quid for that shit about Elton?'
'Yes.'
'Interesting,' he says.
'Who are you? What paper do you work for?'
'I'm John Boyce. I'm Freelance.'

—

Back at the paper. I seek Joan's advice.
'Silly boy.'
'Do I 'fess up?'
'Shouldn't bother, Lynx. No one else round here admits their fuck-ups. Least of all the editor.'
'But I can't sweep this under the carpet?? Our picture's going to be printed in the *Mirror* tomorrow.'

'News moves fast; just pray the story moves on.'
'ATTENTION ATTENTION!'
...Petrie marching down the rows of desks,
'CLUSTERFUCK ALERT!! THE ENEMY HAVE TRACKED DOWN AMERICAN BARRY. JOAN, CAN YOU HANDLE THIS ONE? The *Mirror*'s outside his door. Get Barry out of the country before he cracks and we lose our exclusive.'
'Well, come along, Lynx... '

—

We're inside American Barry's council house off the A4 in Twyford.
It's hell.
The doorbell is ringing constantly.
Steve Pink has taped it down in an effort to make American Barry answer the door, and is tossing business cards and insults through the letterbox.
'...whatever they're offering you, American Barry, we'll pay double.'
It's alarming, but Joan seems remarkably relaxed.
She's crooning to American Barry, while placing a blanket over his head.
'You need to wear this, darling. We can't have them sneaking any more pictures of you. We're sending you to a five-star secret location in Spain for two months, so scum like this can't find you.'
'What do you want me to do?' I ask.
'Make sure the *Mirror* doesn't follow us! And DON'T disappoint me, Lynx.'

As I step out of the house, I see Steve Pink waiting in his car. He's parked directly behind Joan; ready to follow.
He recognises me; winds down his window to jeer: 'Thanks for the photo; we're running it tomorrow.'
I lean in to his open car window: 'Are you proud? You could get me the sack.'
'Are you proud, standing up a pack of lies to save your editor's face?'
'Well, twelve million readers think my work's okay. Remind me, what's the *Mirror*'s circulation figures?'

Before he can answer, he clocks Joan and Blanketed Barry sneaking out of the house.
They're nearly at her car, when Pink says, 'Well, it's been nice chatting, some of us have got work to do – '
Which is my cue to reach through the window, and steal Pink's key –
'OI!' yells Pink.

Before he can react,
I rush to Joan's car –
leap in the passenger seat –
'DRIVE, JOAN! DRIVE!!'
Joan sets off faster than an F1 driver.
As she screeches round the corner, I show her Pink's keys, and she purrs, 'Oh my God, Lynx!... I see great potential in you.'

In the mirror – the *Mirror* – standing in the middle of the road, shaking his fist helplessly as he shrinks far behind. Into irrelevance.

—

In Australia, Elton has been trying to laugh the allegations off. When a local journalist asks him to comment on the kinky sex allegations, he quips, 'Bondage? I thought that was a beach in Sydney.'

But are people laughing with him – or at him? Mud seems to be sticking...
A lucrative contract with Cadbury's has been cancelled –
and Scotland Yard have begun an investigation.

He MUST fly back home.
Partly to celebrate his fortieth... But mainly to clear his name.

His doctors insist he mustn't fly.
The dry air of the flight won't be good for his throat.
But he WILL defy their orders.

He breaks the journey, stopping in LA, to minimise the damage to his throat.
But much of the good work is undone by a call from his mother:

'Reg?'
'It's ELTON, Mum. Mum, you mustn't call, I need to rest my voice.'
'Sorry, Reg. But I'm at the end of my tether. I've had journalists ringing my doorbell, photographers in my garden, people following me everywhere…'
'Imagine what it's like for me. I'm tearing my hair out…'
'Is it worth it? All this fuss? What would happen if you gave them what they wanted?'
'What? – admit to something I didn't do??'
'It would put an end to all this nonsense, Reg.'
'It might also put an end to my career?'
'What is your career worth, if it's this?'
'But I'm good at it?'
'There are other jobs, you know! The neighbour's boy is a dentist. He's done ever so well for himself.'
'I don't want to be a dentist!'
'It's very well-paid, you know.'
'Mum! I'm in *The Times*' Top One Hundred Rich List!'
'AND he gets to see his mother every weekend.'
'I'd like to see the neighbour's boy sell out the Hollywood Bowl doing his bloody root canals.'
'No need to be rude, Reg.'
'Mum. I'm trying to work out what role to play for the next forty years of my life – and at the moment it's Mr Dildo-Twirling-Leather-Pants.'

He slumps back on the floor in despair.
Lies on his back, at one with the carpet.
The ceiling of the Presidential Suite seems a hundred miles away.
Then he sees it…
The metallic blob under the breakfast counter.
He gets up. Looks closer.
It's a recording device.

—

I'm hiding in the toilets at work.
If they can't find me, they can't sack me.
The *Mirror* has printed our photo of American Barry, and I'm wondering how long I can survive in here without food and water.

A sudden bang on the cubicle door.
'Lynx, are you in there?'
'No.'
'Come out, you silly boy...'
'Have you seen the *Mirror*?'
'The *Mirror*'s been upstaged.'
She makes a copy of the *Daily Star*, another of our rivals, limbo-dance under the cubicle door.
The Headline: 'EXPOSED. The Worm who turned on Elton'.
They've uncovered naked pictures of American Barry in a copy of an old underage-porn mag.
'Read it and learn, Lynx. That is a masterpiece of investigative journalism. The reporters who found that deserve to be given a Pulitzer.'
'The reporters who found that deserve to be given a prison cell. Shouldn't we be investigating people who own seriously dodgy porn mags?'
'You'd end up investigating half of Fleet Street... Come out, Lynx. The story's moved on.'

With trepidation, I enter the newsroom – hoping I may have got away with this...
Suddenly: my name, terrifyingly amplified by Petrie's megaphone.
'LYNX! WHERE IS LYNX?!!!'
'Er, yes?'
'I've just had the news editor of the *Mirror* screaming at me for half an hour, because you stole one of their journalist's car keys? Is it true???'
'Er yes. I'm really sorry, I – '
He shakes my hand, 'Fucking brilliant, son – I'm giving you a short-term contract.
Now get your arse down to Gatwick – Elton's flight's due in at four.'

—

The Arrivals Hall, Gatwick.
The press pack are out in force; many recognise me from the Apollo Club, and take the piss by placing drinks orders.
'Another pint of IPA and a packet of pork scratchings, please.'

I smile falsely, wondering how long I will have to endure their mockery –
when suddenly they fall silent.
And I look up – and I see him.
For the first time:
Elton.
...He's magnificent.
Dressed in black and white – top hat and tails.
Flickering in the flashes like a silent movie.
He has a glow; a radiant presence buffed by a million gawps of wonder.
Now, suddenly everyone is busy.
'Over here, Mr John!!'
'Oi, ELTON!'
...Ignored, they try provocation:
'ELTON! Fucked any rent boys lately?'
The chase begins.
Elton's quick – his pursuers weighed down by camera gear.
But I'm young enough, fast enough, to get close enough, to ask:
'Looking forward to your fortieth birthday party?'
He throws tight-jawed anger at the photographers, 'I am looking forward to shaking off these Animals.'
The insult amuses the paps, who play up to it, bleating, hooting and mooing.
But I don't laugh.
As Elton slams the limo door in my face, I see the complex emotions in his eyes: he's hunted – haunted. Frightened.
Mocked by farmyard noises.

—

Back in the newsroom, writing up my copy.
I have a headline:
'The Bitch is Back!!'
But I feel no pride... The memory of those hunted eyes.
'Joan, I feel bad about this.'
'Toughen up, Lynx. I'm sure he's crying into his millions.'

Suddenly: Kelvin... roaring onto the newsroom floor, like a hungry Jurassic beast.
...'TWENTY MILLION QUID...???'

As one, the news floor dips their heads into their work, trying to look busy.
'TWENTY MILLION QUID??? TWENTY MILLION FUCKING QUID??? Have you seen this bogroll??'
He's holding the *Mirror*.
Elton's given them an exclusive interview, saying 'Twenty million damages won't be enough'.
'FUCK ME! This Elton business is no longer a "ferret". It's far more vicious than that... Joan?? What's nastier than a fucking ferret – '
'A Fucking Honey Badger, Kelvin.'
'What's the Fucking collective noun of Fucking Honey Badgers?'
'A Fucking "Colony".'
'It's a Fucking Colony of Fucking Honey Badgers! Right! If Elton wants a fight – we give him a fight. We put a team on this!'
'How big?'
'A dozen. Twelve good men and true. A jury to deliver the verdict of "Guilty".'

And with that, he snatches both my copy and the photo; sees Elton in his top hat and tails... and scribbles a new headline: 'Putting on the Writs'.

—

While the rest of the team goes to pump their vice contacts, I'm to report on Elton's fortieth.

Elton has said his fortieth celebrations will be 'nothing special'. Just a quiet night in with a few friends at dinner.

I'm stood outside the gates whilst three hundred and fifty people arrive;
including Her Royal Highness, Sarah Ferguson, Duchess of York, and Prince Andrew, Ringo, George, Phil Collins, Eric Clapton, Bob Geldof, Lionel Richie and the entire Watford football team.

There's a huge fireworks display. Fabulous ice sculptures. Lobsters, caviar, free-flowing champagne, an enormous cake-the-size-of-a-sarcophagus. There's even a guest performance by Bobby Davro.

The press pack are in good spirits; it's easy for them. They're getting plenty of copy.
They can write about the glamour, the glitz... 'who's wearing what', 'who's in', 'who's out'.

But I'm uneasy.
My paper insists Elton is the enemy; Kelvin will want me to monster him.
But what else CAN you write?? This party is amazing.

I find a payphone, and call Joan with my copy.
'Captain Fantastic Elton John put the glam into glam rock last night with a dazzling fortieth birthday celebration...'
'Whoa, whoa. Stop, Lynx. It'll never get printed. Kelvin doesn't want to hear about "Captain Fantastic" – he wants the "Brown Dirt Cowboy".'
'But this is amazing; it's like Disneyland??'
Joan, in calm tones. 'Never forget who you are writing for.'
'Right: Kelvin.'
'No!! The reader: the ordinary Joe on the street.'
'But Joe might like a bit of glamour, a bit of escapism?'
She chuckles.
'Doubt it. There are three million people unemployed out there. If Joe is not on the dole already, he's worried he's next. How does he feel about a squillionaire eating a cake costing more than his annual income?'
A firework explodes over the ground. A grand illumination, like an idea.
'Great. Yes. I know what to do...'

...I write of decadence, excess and decay.

Elton's agent, Beryl, has bought Elton a Ferrari.
I scratch my typewriter's keys down the sides of it.
The headline: 'EIGHTY-THOUSAND-POUND GIFT FOR ELTON'.
I spread verbal manure on the flower arrangements.
Direct hot fury at the ice sculptures.
And blow the noisy fireworks to pieces.

But what clinches it for Kelvin is when I call Elton a 'Pudgy Piano-Pounder'.

He laughs and laughs. 'I fucking love it!'
And I feel giddy with the thrill of achievement...
...of pleasing this ferocious man with his impossible standards.
And I want more.
...I want more.
'PRINT IT!'

—

Sitting on the Tube to work, seeing the headline.
My headline.
My byline on the front pages.
I want to seize my fellow commuters by their shoulder pads and say: 'See that name?? See that? That's me!!'
I want to snatch the page from the person next to me and autograph it.
I want them to know, I want them to know – that those sooty smears on their fingers – are my words.
The train pulls into Wapping.
I've arrived.

—

Elton reads the article, and immediately phones Bernie.
'Ey up, Elton.'
'Am I fat, Bernie?'
'You could lose a couple of pounds, but I wouldn't say FAT, exactly.'
'Then why are they calling me a "pudgy piano-pounder"?'
Snorts.
'What was that noise?'
'Er, the cat.'
'It's not funny.'
'It is A BIT funny.'
'I'm not laughing. I'm sick of all this bad press! I've got to shift the narrative from decadence and imagined rent-boy sex; back to music.'
'How are you going to do that, old chum?'
'I've been offered an AIDS charity gig at Wembley Arena, I'm thinking I might accept it.'
'You silly plonker; it's too soon! You might damage your voice

and ruin your career.'
'If I don't do something soon – there won't be a career.'

So he nervously steps into the fierce lights of Wembley Arena.
Unsure of the reaction.
Hiding behind thick sunglasses.
The roar which greets him is strange: disembodied, animal, faceless.
Impossible to see the crowd through the dark of his lenses.
He sits at the piano.
One song to change the narrative. One song to appeal to the public's kindness.
'This next song means a lot to me... it's called... "Will You Still Love Me Tomorrow?".'
He plays, tries his voice.
It's frail and pained, cracked and strained. Makes unfamiliar sounds.
At the end of the song, he hunches over the keyboard.
Then he stands before a wall of noise. It's like a waterfall in the dark.
And he extends his arms in the shape of a crucifix.
Was it enough?

The after-show party.
Everyone who's anyone is here... actors, rockers, royalty.
'The Queen's here!' screams Boy George.
Elton turns round, 'Where?'
'I meant you, you pillock. They loved you, Elton!'
'Did they? I couldn't see them?'
Duchess of York, Sarah Ferguson across the room.
Elton catches her eye; she looks away hurriedly. Pretends she was fascinated by what DJ Mike Smith has to say. He knows she's faking because nobody's interested in what DJ Mike Smith has to say.
He hurries across the room, 'Sarah! Sarah.'
She bows her head, won't meet his gaze.
'Please, don't stand near me. There are photographers. I can't be seen with you; Prince Philip gave me a massive bollocking for being seen at your party.'
'Why?'

'Because... We're the Royal Family. We have to be squeaky clean. Can't have a whiff of scandal...'
She disappears into the night, 'They were going to give you a knighthood, you know.'
Leaving Elton, a victim of forfeiture, mouthing words into thin air.

—

Another day.
New pages must be filled.
Can't rest on my laurels; you're only as good as your last story.
Despite long days and late nights, I must be at work by nine.
It's hard, and I need substances to keep going.
...And yes, I am aware of the irony of slagging off Elton for debauched excess, whilst snorting lines to stay awake.

In the newsroom, Kelvin snatches the megaphone off Petrie, and yells: 'WHERE'S THAT CUNT LYNX?'
...Shit. What have I done now?
'Just spoke to a bloke called John Boyce. He knows you.'
'Boyce...?? The Man with the Goatee Beard, from the Apollo?'
'He's an ex-rent boy, knows everybody on the circuit. He's offering to interview the lads who say they've slept with Elton... But he isn't a journalist, so I thought I'd ask *someone skilled* to write them up... Anyway, she wasn't available. So I thought I'd send you instead. Hahaha. Get your arse to Manchester... And bring the results to me.'
I'm troubled.
But Joan smiles: 'You've arrived. He called you a "cunt". That means he thinks you're good.'

—

Boyce has set up a makeshift studio in a room at the Piccadilly Hotel.
When I enter, he immediately rewards me with a bulging Sainsbury's bag.
'What's this, Boyce?'
'Tapes, and affidavits. Done thirty already. Another twenty to do today.'
'Thirty?? Sounds a lot?'

While he sets up the camera, I slip one of the cassette tapes into my Walkman.
Unease.
The testament's Too Wordy; the delivery: lifeless and clumsy. As if read off a card.

The first interviewee of the day is a lad called Wizz. He has an 'Appetite for Destruction' T-shirt.
Track marks up his arm. Hollow eyes.
He shuffles in front of the camera.
'What do you want me to say?'
Boyce hands him a card: '…That you fucked Elton. And he twirled a dildo like Cleopatra… ACTION.'
'I fucked Elton. And he was twirling a dildo like Cleo Laine.'
I can't listen any more: 'Are you actually a rent boy, Wizz?'
'No!!!'
'You do know you could be sued for this?
Elton's suing us for twenty million. You could be next.'
For the first time, his eyes focus.
He turns to Boyce: 'Can I withdraw my statement?'
Boyce's nostrils flare: 'Too late. You've signed the statement. You've spilled out your guts on camera.'
'I'm not comfortable with this,' I growl.
Boyce rounds on me. 'What do you fucking care? You get your byline; everyone's getting paid.'
'I have professional integrity. I'm a journalist.'
He chuckles. 'If you're not going to report the lies of a rent boy, you're at the wrong fucking paper, mate.'
I take the bulging bag of tapes.
The weight bleaching and stretching the wrinkled handles to breaking point.

—

Before my dad went on that fateful trip to South Africa, I asked: 'Why become a journalist, Dad, when it's so dangerous?'
'The work's important, son, you are the eyes and the ears of the public. Their defence against the abuses of power.'
When he'd gone, I swished and swirled the sword in the garden, feeling proud.

Imagining I was a hero – a journalist – fighting the abuse of power.
The sword feels heavy in my hand.
What he never mentioned, what I never imagined, was: what if it was the journalists abusing the power?

—

Back at my desk, the bulging Sainsbury's bag remains unopened.
I can't just write them up; I can't.
Decide to research Boyce's background. Put in a few calls.
What I learn is shocking.
And take the results to Joan.
A bad time. She's on the phone, in the middle of a negotiation.
'...So you have a sex act, a full-frontal nude, and a picture with a young man? I think we can stretch to ten thousand pounds for the three.'
'Joan??'
'I'm busy, Lynx. I'm trying to persuade one of Elton's ex-lovers to sell us his private pictures.'
'This is important, Joan? Boyce is not just a rent boy – he's had nine criminal convictions of fraud.'
'...Your point being...?'
'Well, he's not credible, and he's the source for all this.'
'Of course he's not a saint. But if you want to know what's going on in the sleazy world of male prostitution, there'd be no point asking a vicar, would there?... Actually, probably not true; there's one or two I know who – '
'Boyce is a crook, Joan.'
'And how did you find out he had a criminal record?'
'...I, er... I know a dodgy copper who accessed the national criminal database.'
'Uh-huh.'
'Okay, I'm not proud of that, but – '
' – diamonds are found in dirt, Lynx. Write them up.'

So I type them up, and deliver the dossier of dirty diamonds directly to Kelvin.
He reads them with one eyebrow raised,
'Are these stories all true?'

'Yes,' I squirm. 'Although I'm not sure about the "Cleo Laine" bit.'
'Hn... And you checked them?'
'Yes.'
'Think they're good stories?'
'At least double ferrets.'
There's a savage glint in his unblinking eyes, as he unfurls the phrase:
'You fucking CUNT!'
I now know he has two uses of the word... And this one isn't affectionate.
'In fact you're worse than a CUNT... What's the collective noun of CUNTS?? – it's a "Lynx". You are the Lynx of fucking cunts! Look at the Fucking *Mirror*!'
He thrusts the front page of the *Daily Mirror* into my face.
'I LIED ABOUT ELTON. A teenage boy says he lied about a gay affair with Elton John because he wanted money.'
It's Wizz... panicked by the prospect of legal action, he's admitted lying about Elton to Boyce for five hundred pounds cash.
Suddenly Kelvin rips the paper away, and he's spraying me with spittle.
'Think you're good, eh? Think you're some kind of fucking journalist?? Your work stinks stronger than your fucking aftershave – '
From behind us, a saviour: 'Kelvin darling, you seem uptight...'
It's Joan...
'...somebody needs to give you a bloody good blowjob.'
Kelvin's bollocking has been derailed; Joan is perhaps the only person in Britain that can make Kelvin squirm.
'Joanie, I'm busy.'
'Perhaps I could give you a spectacular blowjob right here.'
He looks absolutely terrified...
...Until she lays the photo of a very famous man, indulging in a sex act on his desk.
'What the... Is that HIM??'
'And here he is, nude...'
'Where'd you get these?'

'These are the no-longer-private photographs of Elton's former lover.'
'Fucking Joanie!!!! I LOVE YOU!!'

My bollocking forgotten, I choose this moment to back out of his office...
...leaving Kelvin salivating on a Scoop.

—

Next day —

'ELTON PORN PHOTO SHAME.'
The full-frontal nude appears on the front page.
The second photo — of Elton cuddling a young man —
in the middle pages.
But the third, says the paper, is too inappropriately sexual for 'a family newspaper'.
...Ironic, considering there's a heavy-breasted naked girl on page three.

Kelvin writes an editorial for the front page. Something which he usually reserves for national disasters:

'In February, *The Sun* published a series on Elton's lifestyle. Elton's reply was volcanic. It was LIES he said and threatened to sue *The Sun* for twenty million.
Other papers, less concerned with the truth than their dreadful circulation figures, tried to take advantage by supporting his campaign against us.

Then we received fresh evidence in the shape of pornographic pictures showing Elton involved in a sex act with a young man.

The Sun has no hard feelings towards Elton John... But he must stop telling lies about *The Sun*. In return we shall stop telling the TRUTH about him.'

He nods in satisfaction.
'PRINT IT!'

—

When the story comes out, Elton retreats to his bedroom.
The door is locked.
Curtains are drawn.
Meals are left outside his bedroom door, which go cold, uneaten.

But he does seek some comfort in food.
In his private fridge, he keeps tubs of peanut butter ice cream and pots of cockles.
He eats them together – a dreadful mix which not even Heston Blumenthal would attempt.

Shovelling and shovelling with a spoon.
Then throws it all up.
Then does it again... Shovelling and shovelling and throws it all up...

He knows it's wrong.
But he does it anyway.
Because his food intake – is the one thing he can control.

And now he places a bottle of sleeping pills. On the table.
Sits staring at the child safety cap.
Imagining the peace within.

Then he cries and cries.
And laughs and laughs.
Staring at the cap.
Wondering...

Does Life begin – or does Life end – at forty?

Suddenly – a knock.
'Mr John?? You've got a visitor. A Mr Michael Parkinson.'
This time, Elton answers the door.

—

MacKenzie is in a good mood; his beloved Millwall beat Bournemouth at the weekend, and now look unlikely to be relegated.
Feet on the desk in his office, he sings a cheery refrain,
'Millwall – super Millwall – no one likes us, we don't care.'
The mailman enters carrying a huge postbag.

'What's this? Fan mail, or writs from Elton's lawyer?'
'Readers' complaints,' says the mailman. 'About your harsh treatment of Elton.'
'Fuck off!! Seriously???... People only think it's harsh cos they like his music. If he was Haircut 100, no fucker would write in.'

He carries on singing – albeit less tunefully than before.
'Millwall, super Millwall – '
Then Accounts enter, looking ashen. 'Bad news, Kelvin. We lost two hundred thousand readers the day of "Porn Photo Shame".'
'Can't be right?? That was a fucking ferret?'

He summons Petrie. 'Why's everyone getting behind Elton?'
'I THINK YOU'RE COMING ACROSS AS A BULLY?'
'Who's saying that? – I'll fucking twat them.'
'*Everyone*. The Public like Elton: he's stayed in Britain, pays his taxes, loves his footie. He's one of us.'
'He's one of THEM.'
'People don't care, Kelvin – he's a great entertainer.'
'*We're* the great entertainers: *The* fucking *Sun*! ME. US – does he have TWELVE MILLION READERS?!'
'Um. Well, he's got three hundred million listeners... That's how many records he's sold.'
'Yeah, but does he actually speak to the public?'
'He's about to be interviewed by Michael Parkinson.'
For once, Kelvin is silenced.
Michael Parkinson hosts the country's favourite chat show. Its viewership is similar in number to *The Sun*'s readership.
Elton will have a platform. A voice. A POWERFUL voice.
'FUCK. We need to get into that audience. Find out what's said.'

—

I'm standing in a car park in Leeds, because Parkinson records his shows at Yorkshire Television.
I can't get into the recording – none of the press pack can – Journalists are banned, because Elton wants to 'control the narrative for a change'.

I try to blag my way in.
Produce ID from my wallet, and thrust it into the doorman's face, saying confidently:

'Security. Need to check the auditorium. Have had word some journalists have infiltrated the audience.'
'Can't let you in.'
'Why?'
'Because that's not a security pass; it's a Young Person's Railcard.'
'Come on, do us a favour, let us in.'
He considers a moment, says: 'I tell you what you can do: you can travel on trains for discounted prices.'
And laughs uproariously at his own joke.
Fuckwit.

I'm loitering, waiting for the recording to end, so I can grab some quotes from the studio audience.
My only crumb of comfort – Steve Pink's there, too. He couldn't get in either.
He nods in acknowledgement, hands tucked into his armpits against the Yorkshire cold.
He smirks warily, 'Watch your car keys, fellas! Here comes *The Scum*.'
'Morning Steve.'
'Surprised *The Sun* are here, actually. Thought you'd stay in London – cos you're going to make it all up anyway.'
'Surprised the *Mirror* are here, actually. You're usually late on every story. There was a war which ended in 1945 – you covered that one yet?'
'Touché, my friend.'
He blows into his cupped hands. 'This is the life, eh? When I got into this job, I wanted to be the next Woodward or Bernstein; taking down presidents and defending the masses. Instead, we're stood in a car park dishing dirt on a "pudgy piano-pounder".'
'It sells papers.'
'We're not "papers"! We're *NEWS*papers.'

Before I can answer, the doors are thrust open, and the audience spray out.
I'm first to pounce, pressing the punters for answers.
The mood: sour.
I appear to be invisible.
A few 'accidental' shoulders. An elbow.

'Can you tell *The Sun* readers what Elton said?'
'Fuck off.'
'Was that what Elton said? Or is that your personal message to *The Sun* readership?'
No answer.
I ask an elderly man:
'Would you mind giving me a statement?'
'Yeah,' says Granddad, 'I'll give you a statement. You people are scum.'
'I'm just doing my job, sir.'
'The Free Press isn't just Free to write anything, you know.'
'It IS a Democracy, mate.'
'Who wants to read what people do in the privacy of their own homes?'
'Er, twelve million readers.'
Suddenly a huge gobbit of spit in my eye.
'What was that for?'
The crowd bubbling, hot and dangerous.
A woman yelling: 'You just make it all up.'
'Wish I did make it up; wish I was in my office, making up stories, instead of talking to you, you sour-faced Yorkshire trout.'
Bang! I'm thumped in the face.
'Cheeky twat!'
'SORRY.'
Another blow.
'I'm sorry I'm sorry.'
Anger: deaf to entreaty.
Cowering.
As the blows fall.
Sinking in a quicksand of fury.
PAAAAAPPP!
– the sudden long blare of a car horn.

A moment of distraction.
Enough to push out of the crowd.
The car: driven by Steve Pink.
The door: open.
'GET IN.'
I jump in.
Lock.

Now: faces and fury
...fists on the roof
...The car is shaken on its axle.
But carefully, slowly, he pulls away.

We drive in silence.
I've long wiped the spittle from my face – but can still feel its ghostly presence on my cheek.
'Thanks. If you hadn't picked me up, I think they might have lynched me.'
'Lucky no one had nicked my car keys, today.'
'Ha.'
I prod the pulp of my throbbing eye.
'Breaks my heart, Lynx. When I got into this job, Journalists had respect... Watched *Spitting Image* this weekend – and we were portrayed as Pigs.'
'Oink oink.'
'It's Rupert Murdoch and Bloody Robert Maxwell's fault, with their bingo and tits and celebrity fuckfests.'
'People want Escapism, not News, Steve; Life's depressing enough. We're in the Entertainment business.'
'You think your paper's "entertainment"?? Have you READ your paper's editorials?'
'Not really.'
'You *should*.'
'Why's it matter so much to you?'
'Just read them. You'll see.'
Drives on in silence.
Then places his hand on my thigh.

—

I return to the newsroom with a black eye.
Joan seems thrilled. 'Did Elton do that?? Seems Tuesday night was alright for fighting.'
MacKenzie pushes through.
He's worried, properly worried – but not for me.
'What the fuck happened in that recording?'
'I dunno, Kelvin. There's a lot of anger out there.'

—

Still ignorant of the contents of the show, MacKenzie launches a fiery defence the day of the broadcast.
A hostile front page, titled: 'Fairy Tales'.
'*The Sun* urges its twelve million readers to sit down and watch Elton John's performance on the Michael Parkinson show. Not since Vivien Leigh in *Gone with the Wind* has there been such an extraordinary piece of acting... If you believe Elton, you'll believe in fairies.'

That night, tins of beer in hand, the news team crowds around the TV... watching the show along with twelve million others.
After a nasal introduction from the Yorkshire David Frost, Elton enters.
No glitz, no glamour. No sequins, no wigs. Drably dressed.
Not playing the star, not today.
He's one of us.
He says the '*Sun* allegations are all lies'.
Tells of the relentless pursuit by the press pack,
the bug in his hotel suite,
the paranoia and the loss of friends,
the harassment which forced his mother to flee the country.
...The suicidal feelings.

I shudder.
Till now, we've treated Elton as a cartoon character.
Two-dimensional. Hardly real.
But now, beneath all the costumes and the wigs – The Real Person.
And now a voice.
A persistent, nagging voice.
Constantly in my head like tinnitus.
It's Pink's.
'You should read your own paper's editorials...'

I go downstairs to the archive. Pull out the papers for the past year.
Scan the editorials.
The intolerance and homophobia is shocking.
'Gay Plague',
'Gay and Wicked',

'Gays only have themselves to blame for AIDS',
'treat these perverts with the contempt they deserve',
'the Gays have to Shut Up',
'A man or woman with AIDS is a timebomb, a menace to all society',
'Fly away gays and we will pay'.
And I realise.
This battle we're engaged in – is much bigger than Elton John and MacKenzie...
This is the fight for the soul of a nation.

—

July twenty-fourth: a turning point.
Tory Party chairman, Jeffrey Archer, successfully sues the *Daily Star* for half a million.
It's a massive sum.
In context, you'll get around twenty thousand pounds if you lose an eye in an industrial accident.

And this giant payout isn't a one-off.
Carmen Proetta – who they called 'The Tart of Gibraltar' – unsurprisingly sued for a hundred and fifty k.
Then Koo Stark sues the *Sunday People* for twice that.
Clearly the courts are sending the press a message. 'Truth has a high value.'

That night – one a.m.
Kelvin can't sleep.
Kelvin knows that the paper's owner, Rupert Murdoch, will put up with anything – except losing money.

If Archer was awarded half a million for false allegations – what would Elton expect?
The *Star*'s editor has been sacked – surely Kelvin will suffer a similar fate?

The phone rings.
Only one person ever calls at this time of night: Murdoch himself.
Kelvin braces himself. He's used to lengthy bollockings; this surely will break all records.

'Hello, boss.'
'Are we alright on this Elton business, Kelvin?'
'Yes.'
Click.

The brevity is chilling.

—

Next morning, Joan gives me a warning. 'Don't fuck up today, Lynx. Don't be Kelvin's lightning rod.'
When Kelvin enters the newsroom floor, everybody has their heads down, typing frantically.
'FUCK!!! What's more ferocious than a honey badger??!'
'A sabre-toothed tiger, Kelvin... And before you ask, it's an "Ambush" of Sabre-Toothed Tigers.'
'This is all that fucking rent boy's fault! If it wasn't for him – none of this would have happened.'
No one dares tell Kelvin he might share the blame.
'Is he still in Spain?? Hn?? Living it up at our expense?? Drinking our beer and eating our lobster? FUCK HIM!! Bring him home. Cut him off.'
'I'll book him a flight, Kelvin.'
'FUCK HIM!! Let him make his own way home.'
Then he turns to the newsroom:
'And you lot had better bring Elton down – or you'll be fucking out next!'
Joan turns to me, 'Follow Elton everywhere. Don't let him out of your sight.'

—

So I find myself chasing Elton's limo round town, from meeting to meeting.
Hating my paper, mentally preparing my resignation notice...

And then, Elton drives to Heathrow Airport.
I stand behind him at the check-in, I see his luggage tagged to New York.
Phone the newsdesk.
'He's getting onto Concorde! What do I do?'
'Follow him! Don't let him out of your sight.'

'But it's Concorde!'
'My dear, you have a lot to learn about expense accounts. Has anybody else followed him?'
'Don't think so.'
'Buy every seat in first class, just in case – make sure no one gets to sit next to him.'

So I follow Elton onto Concorde.
For four hours I sit in the seat behind him, drinking way too much complimentary champagne.

I'm quite drunk when we get to New York.
Change flights, go to Chicago.
Where can he be going??
I get to jump into a cab and say 'Follow that limo!!'

Then doze off on the back seat, as we drive all the way to Indiana.
To a town called Cicero.

The driver wakes me, when we pull up in tree-lined American suburbia.
It's the fall...
Naked branches exposed like truths.

Elton gets out of his limo – walks up to a humble, white, weatherboard house.
And knocks on the door.

It's opened by a young man.
Barely adult. Pale, handsome.
The teenager shrieks.
Leaps into Elton's arms. Clings to him fiercely.
They hold the embrace warmly. For a long time.
Oh my.
There's love here.
Shit, I don't have a camera.
The boy shows him into the house.
Shuts the door.

Wow. Wow.

MacKenzie's instincts were right:
Elton and young boys.

I hurriedly start writing my copy. If I can knock something out quickly, it might make the late editions.

'ELTON'S DIRTY SECRET... Rocker Elton jetted to America yesterday, for a secret tryst with a handsome young man...'

I race down the main street to a photocopy shop with a fax. The storekeeper's a good old boy with a face like a pumpkin. Works slowly terribly slowly.

'Can you send this fax right now, please.'

'Well yessir.'

Am irritated as he takes my pages, and very very carefully lines up the corners, asking:

'You from England?'

'Yeah. Can't imagine you see many Brits out here.'

'We get English. That Elton John comes out here.'

He places my pages in the guide rails of the machine.

'Oh, really?'

'Such a kind man. The way he looks after Ryan.'

He dials *The Sun*'s fax number.

'Ryan?'

'Ryan White. Lives in the white weatherboard house. He was a haemophiliac. He got AIDS through a blood transfusion. People treated him so bad, and Elton heard – so he tries to make his life nicer before he dies.'

The fax line connects.

The machine grinds horrific noises, as the copy prepares to roll through.

The itch, the urge.

To wash my hands.

I snatch the copy out of the tray before the pages roll into the machine.

'Sir, it hasn't sent yet?'

'Don't worry. I need to check my story first.'

—

I knock on the door of Ryan White's house and ask to speak to Elton John.

And now the Rocketman stands before me. Suspicious.

'You! You were the guy on the plane, who spent the flight drinking all the free champagne and staring at the back of my head. What do you want?'
'I want to say sorry. For my part in this. We've been accusing you of selfishly exploiting young men for sex. But the reality is, you're kind; *kind* to this young man, when the world's been cruel. I want to write about you and Ryan – set the record straight.'
'I am NOT going to use Ryan to prop up my image.'
'Okay. Okay, I won't write about it.'
'How can I trust you? How can I trust any of you?'
'You have my word.'
He shuts the door in my face.

I'm as good as my word. I don't write the story up.
But I DO do the unthinkable.
I call American Barry...

After months of paella and payola, American Barry is back in Twyford –
His savings fading faster than his tan.
No longer does he eat lobster meals from fine bone china...
It's back to fish suppers wrapped in newspapers.
When the phone rings, he licks his cod and chips from his grease-stained fingers.
'Hello?'
'Hi, Barry. It's Lynx from *The Sun*.'
'Fuck off.'
'Don't put the phone down! Hear me out!'
'Don't want to hear from *The Sun* no more – '
' – Elton is a second dad to a kid with AIDS.'
A pause.
'...Talk to me.'
I tell him the Rocker and Ryan's story.
At the end he says quietly, 'Why are you telling me this?'
'You know why.'
'Yes,' he says quietly.
Many of Barry's rent-boy colleagues had caught the disease.
And were disowned by their communities, their friends and families.

But not by Elton, the man he could have destroyed.
'I'm going to give you a number, Barry. You got a pen?'
'Yes.'
Barry licks newsprint and grease from his fingers, tasting a slick of Guilt.
And writes down Steve Pink's number.

—

My first day back from the States – the Tube to work.
The commuters have no faces. Just copies of the *Daily Mirror.*
'Rent boy in pop scandal confesses "MY SEX LIES OVER ELTON".'
Byline: Steve Pink.
It's an exclusive interview with American Barry, who admits he made it all up.
'I only did it for the money and *The Sun* were easy to con. I've never met Elton John... in fact I hate his music. I think Haircut 100 are miles better.'
I feel a pride... It's not my byline, but it's my story; a True Story...

...Kelvin's going to go ballistic.
...It's going to be a day staring intently into the monitors.
The train shrieks to a stop...
'Mind the Gap.'

—

When Kelvin reads the story, he screams.
Sweeps the dossier off his desk. His case has collapsed.
'If I'm going down, I'm taking Elton with me.'
He looks wildly round the newsroom.
'What have we got? What have we got? Anything!'
The team are frozen in fear.
His fierce eyes, his jabbing finger, point at me.
'Lynx! – I sent you all the way to America – didn't you get ANYTHING??'
I'm not going to help him. I shake my head.
'Joan, you must have something. You always have something.'
'I've got a lead, but it needs work, Kelvin...'

'What is it, Joan??'
'One of Elton's staff said he'd had his rottweilers' voice boxes cut out. To make them more effective guard dogs; make them like silent assassins...'
'Brilliant. Write it up!'
'He might have been winding me up. I should check it first.'
'Fuck that, get it written! We're going to FUCK ELTON JOHN!!! Take that fucker down!!!'

When Kelvin has gone, I turn to Joan with horror. 'You're not seriously writing that up?'
'Why not?'
'You can't write up dodgy stories without checking them first. That's what created this mess in the first place.'
'Kelvin wants it; why should I question Kelvin?'
'Because Kelvin is – in Kelvin's words – a cunt.'
'Kelvin is one of the best editors there's ever been.'
'Because he "sells papers"?'
'Because he's a genius. The whole of Fleet Street is trying to copy him; no one can match his headlines – they're as concise as a haiku. Witty, provocative: once read – never forgotten. People will be writing plays about them in forty years' time.'
'But where's the news value?'
'Don't be so pompous, Lynx.'
'This isn't in the Public Interest!'
'Who are you to tell the public what "should and shouldn't" interest them? Hm? What are you: some kind of superior intellect who knows better than everybody else? Fuck off to the *Guardian*, Lynx!'

—

And so Joan writes the penultimate and bizarrest story of this extraordinary tale:
The 'MYSTERY OF ELTON'S SILENT DOGS'.

Which prompts a phone call.
'Did you do it, Reg?'
'It's "Elton", Mum... Did I do "what"?'
'...silence your guard dogs by a horrific operation to stop them barking.'

'No. Because I've only got one dog; it's a poodle. And it's quite yappy.'
'So are you going to sue them about this?'
'I thought you thought I should just "give them what they want"?'
'But Reg – you've got a poodle! Their story's so easy to disprove; *The Sun* CAN'T win! Their entire defence collapses!! You can force them to settle out of court!'
'...oh my God! Mum!! You're a genius!!'

—

The day before the trial, there are some unusual visitors to Wapping.
MacKenzie is on the newsroom floor when Elton and his lawyers sweep through. And enter his office.
Then Murdoch, and the in-house lawyers.
MacKenzie tries to follow. But the door is shut in his face.

Mid-morning the negotiations are still going on.
Kelvin loiters at my desk, 'Do you think I've been harsh on Elton?'
'I've been reading your editorials – I think you're harsh on a lot of people.'
'Ha! You think I edit the paper, don't you? No, no, no. The readers do. They choose the stories. If they don't buy it, we don't write it. Blame me all you want, but there are five million editors.'
'Maybe we should stop giving the readers what they want. And start giving them what they need.'

Just then Murdoch emerges from the meeting with the lawyers, wearing the rictus smile of a corpse.
'How was it, boss?'
'How do you think it was?? I'm paying him a million pounds.'
'Tell him to fuck himself.'
'And he wants an unconditional apology.'
'Okay, we'll bury it on page twenty-four.'
'*On the Front Page*. And a double-page feature saying something nice about him.'
'Yes, boss. I'll come up with something.'

'Oh you won't be writing it.'
'Then who...?'
'Elton's lawyers.'
'But they won't know the house style?'
From the doorway Elton smiles and points to me – 'This helpful young chap will work with them. I trust him.'
MacKenzie's mouth thrashes. But no sounds come out.
The man with the loudest voice in Britain: silenced.
The lawyers edit his paper now.

That's how I co-wrote a splash and spread in *The Sun*.
The front page: 'SORRY ELTON!'
A double-page interview which was so treacly sweet, it should carry a heath warning for diabetics. Saying how Elton had lost weight.

—

Next day, at the celebration party, there's much laughing.
Elton's lawyers joking that, as they're now editors of *The Sun*, everyone's the 'C' word and and every anecdote is a 'ferret'.
I'm one of only two invited journalists; Steve Pink is the other.
I cuff his shoulder.
'Thanks, mate – if it wasn't for you directing me to MacKenzie's editorials – I wouldn't have ended up editing the front page or writing a two-page feature!'
Elton arrives to top up our glasses, and Steve addresses us both.
'Yeah – about your two-page feature. You proud of that?'
'Course.'
'Elton, you wanted everyone to know you "lost two stone by getting fit"? You think that's appropriate??'
Elton is shocked by the aggression.
'Yeah. Nice to get some positive press, for a change.'
'You had control of the nation's narrative for one day: you could have said anything. And you used it to say "you'd lost weight"?? You had THE VOICE. A unique opportunity. You could have said something that MATTERED. Instead you made it all about you... Why are you better than MacKenzie?'
Elton's smile fades.
He looks around the room. Sees the friendly faces of this story.

But then, he sees clearly through the world's most famous lenses.
And realises who's missing.
Ryan.
And now knows what he should have said.
He nods, in answer to an internal question. He knows who to be for the next forty years of his life.
Puts down the bottle.
And quietly leaves his own party.
Like all leaders: alone.

—

Since the events of this story, Elton set up his AIDS Foundation.
It's raised over six hundred millions dollars.
And has played a major part in changing global attitudes.

And he's returned to singing.
He can't hit the high notes of his youth.
The screeching falsettos: cut out with the nodules.
But he has a voice; it's a new voice.
Deeper, richer.
More mature.

Those 1987 tabloid pages are yellow now. Most pulped, rarely seen.

The pages that remain, are hidden like secrets.
In the darkness of our houses.
Found during renovations.
Cobwebbed under floorboards.
Wrapping valuables in dusty attics.
A History, which still leaves a sooty residue.
Now crumbling into irrelevance.

…These days, we don't take our news from the papers;
we no longer read News in black and white.

Now we take it from the internet,
Where the screens have hues and tones and nuance.
Each pixel capable of sixteen million colours…

…too many colours.
Too many Truths.

Next time you read a story you agree with,
And your finger hovers over the retweet or share button,
and you say to yourself: 'it fucking SOUNDS true!'
– remember this:

You are now the editors of the National Narrative.

We are all Kelvin MacKenzie now.

Blackout.

—

A slide as the audience exits, reading:

'Bloody Elton John…

You can't turn on a TV or pick up a paper, right, without seeing the bow-legged fat-boy… I think The Sun *should have its million quid back. It hasn't damaged him at all, has it?… So no, I don't feel bad about him, not at all'*

[*Kelvin MacKenzie, interviewed in the* Press Gazette, *2006*]

A Nick Hern Book

Monstering the Rocketman first published in Great Britain in 2026 as a paperback original by Nick Hern Books Limited, The Glasshouse, 49a Goldhawk Road, London W12 8QP

Monstering the Rocketman © copyright © 2026 Henry Naylor

Henry Naylor has asserted his moral right to be identified as the author of this work

Cover photograph by Rosalind Furlong

Designed and typeset by Nick Hern Books, London
Printed in Great Britain by Mimeo Ltd, Huntingdon, Cambridgeshire PE29 6XX

A CIP catalogue record for this book is available from the British Library

ISBN 978 1 83904 561 5

CAUTION All rights whatsoever in this play are strictly reserved. Requests to reproduce the text in whole or in part should be addressed to the publisher. This book may not be used, in whole or in part, for the development or training of artificial intelligence technologies or systems.

Amateur Performing Rights Applications for performance, including readings and excerpts, by amateurs in the English language throughout the world should be addressed to the Performing Rights Manager, Nick Hern Books, The Glasshouse, 49a Goldhawk Road, London W12 8QP, *tel* +44 (0)20 8749 4953, *email* rights@nickhernbooks.co.uk, except as follows:

Australia: ORiGiN Theatrical, *email* enquiries@originmusic.com.au, *web* www.origintheatrical.com.au

New Zealand: Play Bureau, 20 Rua Street, Mangapapa, Gisborne, 4010, *tel* +64 21 258 3998, *email* info@playbureau.com

United States of America and Canada: United Agents, see details below.

Professional Performing Rights Applications for performance by professionals in any medium and in any language throughout the world (and by amateur and stock companies in the United States of America and Canada) should be addressed to United Agents, 12–26 Lexington Street, London W1F 0LE

No performance of any kind may be given unless a licence has been obtained. Applications should be made before rehearsals begin. Publication of this play does not necessarily indicate its availability for amateur performance.

www.nickhernbooks.co.uk/environmental-policy

Nick Hern Books' authorised representative in the EU is
Easy Access System Europe – Mustamäe tee 50, 10621 Tallinn, Estonia
email gpsr.requests@easproject.com

www.nickhernbooks.co.uk

@nickhernbooks